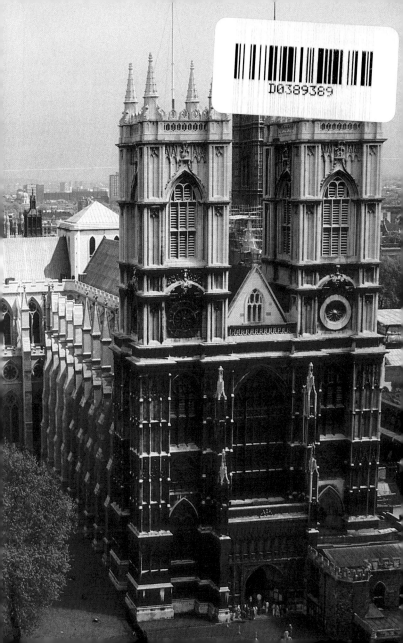

D0389389

First published 28th July 1986

Published by Ladybird Books Ltd Loughborough
Leicestershire UK
Ladybird Books Inc Lewiston Maine 04240 USA

ANDREW SARAH

Royal Wedding

by **AUDREY DALY**

Ladybird Books

A cheeky grin from a small boy

Prince Andrew has always been a favourite with the British public: from the moment they first saw his cheerful grin.

Although he grew up in the solid security of the royal family circle, he has found time for all kinds of adventure – and mischief too (one of his teachers said he was 'a bit of a handful'). He followed his father and his brother Charles to the famous Scottish school of Gordonstoun, noted for its rugged training.

They both were made 'Guardian' (which is what the head boy there is called). Andrew didn't receive this honour. On the other hand, he enjoyed his schooldays (which is more than Prince Charles did).

The royal family at Windsor

4

Prince Andrew rides, skis, shoots, sails, plays rugby, and makes parachute jumps. He was a fully fledged glider pilot before he was sixteen – but the law made him wait until then to fly solo and get his licence

This may have been because by that time there were girls at Gordonstoun as well.

There was never any great discussion about what Andrew was going to be when he left school. There is a tradition in the royal family that the second son of the sovereign always goes into the Royal Navy, and off he went to Dartmouth. And just like every other new recruit he was told, 'Get your hair cut.'

In the course of his hobby of photography, Prince Andrew has had the choice of some of the world's loveliest girls. Now, at twenty six, he has made up his mind – and his bride is a girl he has known since he was four.

Prince Andrew was trained as a helicopter pilot, and flew a Sea King helicopter during the Falklands war. Here he is seen with his helicopter on HMS Brazen. The crew called it 'the brazen hussy'

5

An early photograph of Sarah   *The Princess of Wales is a close friend*

Our newest royal lady has Titian hair, freckles, and a sense of fun. Sarah Margaret Ferguson was born on 15th October 1959, just four months before her bridegroom. She has always been part of the royal family circle, and is in fact distantly related to Andrew. They are sixth cousins once removed. She is also related to another member of the royal family: the Princess of Wales, who is her fourth cousin, and a close friend.

Although Andrew and Sarah have been friends from childhood, no one ever thought they might one day get married. Both have pursued their own careers and interests since leaving school.

Childhood friends
(but not sweethearts!)

Dummer Down House, the Ferguson country home

The bride's coat of arms. The Latin words say, ''Through misfortune to happiness''

Sarah Ferguson works for a graphics design firm which produces illustrated catalogues for such names as Sotheby's, the famous auctioneers of great paintings and antiques. And she is going on with her job – she will be the first royal wife to do so.

The bride's mother, who is now married to an Argentinian professional polo player, Mr Hector Barrantes

On her way to work

Major Ronald Ferguson with his daughters Jane and Sarah – and the dogs

Although they had been friends from childhood, in later years Prince Andrew and Sarah only met from time to time.

Ascot races 1986.

The first change came in June 1985, when Sarah was seen at Ascot with Prince Andrew: as the guest of his mother, the Queen. In December, she was invited to join the royal family on their holiday break.

The photographers woke up, and began to follow her around.

Then she went with the Princess of Wales and young Prince William to visit Andrew on his ship, HMS *Brazen*. Sarah was the newest girlfriend: it looked as if she were going to be the most important.

And so it turned out.

At the Queen's 60th birthday

Mobbed by photographers

The ring – 10 diamonds and a large ruby set in yellow and white gold. Prince Andrew helped to design it

An engagement kiss

On 19th March 1986, the young couple's engagement was announced – they celebrated with pink champagne. Then not long after, we heard that the wedding was to be on 23rd July. A family wedding was planned, in Westminster Abbey, with not nearly as many people as were invited to Prince Charles' wedding.

There were to be, however, 1 800 guests. Not exactly a small wedding!

A formal engagement photograph

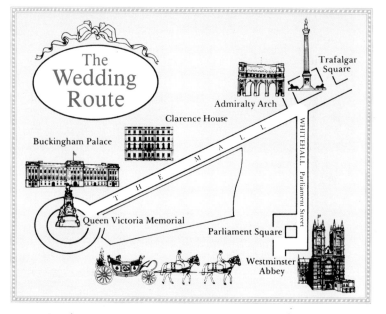

The Wedding Route

Buckingham Palace

Clarence House

Admiralty Arch

Trafalgar Square

THE MALL

WHITEHALL, Parliament Street

Queen Victoria Memorial

Parliament Square

Westminster Abbey

Getting ready for any wedding is always a happy time. Everyone makes a special effort to see that things go well. When a prince gets married however, there are all sorts of extra preparations to be made.

Policemen have to deal with the crowds, and plainclothes security men have to make sure that the route from Buckingham Palace to the Abbey is safe. Westminster Abbey itself must also be checked thoroughly. On 23rd July, there were 1500 police on duty altogether!

A mounted policewoman

The streets must be cleaned, and a carpet laid for the bride to walk on. Very often it is a red carpet, but this time the bride had requested a royal blue one.

The Glass Coach, in which the bride travelled to the wedding

The coaches and carriages to be used in the carriage procession must be cleaned and polished, and the horses groomed to perfection, ready to play their part.

The Royal Mews, where the Queen's carriage horses are kept

Preparing for the wedding

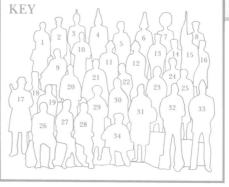

To make the royal wedding day complete in every detail, people with all sorts of different skills were involved, many of them sworn to secrecy about the work they were doing. There was the dress designer... the flower arrangers... the police... the street cleaners... And here they are, the men and women who helped to make it such a success.

1 Lance-Corporal David Garland, *farrier*, was ready with hammer and nails in case one of the 190 horses should shed a shoe.

2 Sergeant Apprentice Simon Haywood, *route-liner*, stood motionless for more than two hours in the gutter of Trafalgar Square, wearing immaculate dress uniform.

3 Junior Technician Paul Williams, *bandsman*, was ready with oboe, clarinet and cymbals to play several National Anthems and a selection of military melodies.

4 Squadron Corporal-Major Rod Flory, *escort*, rode as warrant officer in the Captain's Escort, accompanying Prince Andrew and Prince Edward to the Abbey, and the bride and groom on the return journey.

5 Lance-Bombardier Andrew Evans, *guard*, with the Queen's Life Guard at Horse Guards Arch.

6 Trooper Greg Wood, *escort*, rode in the Sovereign's Escort with the Queen to and from the Abbey.

7 Guardsman Shaun Codd, *route-liner*, was among those standing to attention all through the day.

8 Lance-Corporal Ian Parrott, *route-liner*, at the lower end of Whitehall.

9 Corporal John Perrin, *saddler*, was up at dawn to saddle up the escorts and check the harness before the troop left barracks for the Palace.

10 Lance-Corporal John Valentine, *groom*, was one of those responsible for the impeccable turnout of the horse ridden by the commander of the Sovereign's Escort.

11 Marine Mark Neat, *route-liner*, in Parliament Square.

12 Corporal Bugler Clive Lawton, *musician*, was ready with bugle, flat drum and side drum in his band along the route.

13 Able-Seaman Fred Longman, *usher*, handed out orders of service to guests as they arrived at the Abbey's west door.

14 Wren Lorna Morrissey, *usher*, distributed orders of service.

15 Rodney Meadows, *Abbey bellringer*, led a team of 10 in a 3½-hour full peal after the service.

16 Nurse Anne Arnold, *usher*, was with the orders of service squad at the west door.

17 Chief Cook Trevor Spicer, *baker*, was in charge of making the wedding cake.

18 Sergeant Alan Starling, *baker*, helped to bake the royal wedding cake.

19 Wren Steward Mandy Platt, *food artist*, was in charge of the cake decoration.

20 Keith Webster, *choirboy*.

21 Simon Preston, *Abbey organist*.

22 Emma St John Smith, *Abbey press officer*, checked the credentials of the 250 press and TV personnel allowed inside.

23 Mrs Doris Wellham, *florist*, was in charge of making up the bride's bouquet.

24 Azad Khaleel, *St John Ambulance man*, was on duty inside the Abbey to administer first aid.

25 Miss Marjorie Mudge, *MBE*, *steward*, helped to show the Royal and Ferguson families to their seats.

26 Henry Phillips, *jeweller*, supervised the making of both the engagement and wedding rings for Sarah Ferguson.

27 Lindka Cierach, *dressmaker*, made THE dress.

28 Gordon Jones, *tailor*, made the dress uniforms for the Princes Andrew and Edward.

29 Mrs Marjorie Watling, *flower arranger*, helped to design the Abbey floral decoration.

30 Gene Nocon, *photographer*, assisted official wedding photographer Albert Mackenzie Watson at the formal Palace picture session.

31 Mrs Pam McNicol, *flower arranger*, masterminded setting up the flower displays in the Abbey.

32 Peter Codd, *dustman*, headed the gang of 20 men sweeping the processional route.

33 PC 159E Simon Hobson, *police constable*, was one of hundreds of officers on crowd control duty.

34 Barry Chaston, *television cameraman*, helped to cover the day's events.

By nine o'clock on Wednesday 23rd July 1986, the streets around Buckingham Palace were already full. Some people had even made sure of their places by sleeping on the pavement. A few had been there since Monday!

Everywhere there were smiling expectant faces, some even painted red, white and blue! The air was electric with anticipation.

That was in London. But elsewhere people were

preparing for a festive day as well. Television was going to take them step by step, right beside Andrew, newly created Duke of York, and his bride Sarah, through the wedding of the year. All over Britain – all over the world – people weren't going to miss a minute of it. Something like three hundred million viewers were going to a wedding.

Mounted police, followed by the Sovereign's Escort of the Household Cavalry, heralded the start of the Queen's Carriage Procession. The Queen and Prince Philip were in the first coach. The moment they drove through the Buckingham Palace Grand Entrance gates, the cheers started, and followed them all the way to Westminster Abbey.

The Queen looked lovely in delphinium blue silk and pearls. Prince Philip was of course wearing Naval uniform

Queen Elizabeth the Queen Mother followed in the next coach, with Princess Margaret and her family, Viscount Linley and Lady Sarah Armstrong-Jones. At 85 years old, our much loved Queen Mother was still stealing the show in a flowing silk chiffon dress in her favourite blue, with an ostrich feather hat. Princess Margaret also looked most attractive in blue

Although the cheers were already deafening, they seemed to grow louder as the Prince and Princess of Wales waved on their way past. Fashion leader Princess Diana in a turquoise and black spotted silk dress had a slightly wistful air. Was she remembering her own wedding five short years ago? Prince Charles was smiling cheerfully: no doubt he was delighted that it wasn't his turn this time!

In the fourth coach, Princess Anne and her husband, Captain Mark Phillips, with the Earl of Westmorland, who is Master of the Horse. Princess Anne has always favoured a more tailored approach to fashion. Today, as sister of the bridegroom, she was wearing an elegant dress in daffodil yellow

19

Just after eleven o'clock, the Guard of Honour gave a Royal Salute and the Band played the first bars of the National Anthem as the bridegroom set off for the Abbey.

Prince Edward was with him, to act as his "supporter". When members of the royal family marry, they have a "supporter", rather than a "best man". As in any other wedding, Prince Edward had to make sure that his brother arrived at the church on time, and that the wedding rings were ready at the critical moment in the ceremony.

Prince Andrew was a little more serious than usual on the way to the wedding. Perhaps he was somewhat nervous as nearly all bridegrooms are.

Then, as he arrived at the Abbey, the crowd began to sing, "The Grand Old Duke of York", and he waved a cheery acknowledgment.

At last the moment came — that first glimpse of the bride as she left Clarence House in the fairytale Glass Coach, her father beside her.

The billowing folds of her dress seemed to fill the coach. Her veil was held in place by a circlet of yellow roses, later removed to show a diamond tiara.

Then the carriage pulled up at the West Door of the Abbey and to a storm of pleasure and approval, Miss Sarah Ferguson took her last few steps as a single woman, into Westminster Abbey.

A pause for adjustment to the most talked-of dress
of the year, designed by Lindka Cierach. The dress
was made of ivory duchess satin, sequinned and
embroidered with the bride's coat of arms. The train
was also embroidered with the initials of the bride
and groom, as well as anchors and bumblebees.

The materials used in the bride's and bridesmaids' dresses

One of the dress designer's sketches

25

The awe-inspiring magnificence of the Abbey and the exquisite flower arrangements to be seen everywhere formed a splendid setting. Sarah Ferguson had a quick whispered word with the pages and bridesmaids (her "little people" as she called them). Then they lined up quietly behind her for the start of the bridal procession – four bridesmaids in pretty peach dresses and four pages. They were Zara Phillips, Alice Ferguson, Lady Rosanagh Innes-Ker and Laura Fellowes, and the boys – Prince William, Seamus Makim, Andrew Ferguson and Peter Phillips.

The organist began to play the Imperial March by Edward Elgar, and the bride moved slowly up the aisle on her father's arm.

Miss Ferguson had asked for the old form of service from the 1662 Prayer Book. This includes the words "to obey", and, as she spoke these words at the ceremony she looked up at Andrew mischievously. In an interview she had said that she is prepared to accept her husband's final choice when any moral decision is called for.

Both bride and groom spoke out confidently as they took their vows, although at one point Sarah repeated Andrew's third name.

The ceremony was over and the register had been signed. The new Duchess curtsied to the Queen.

Then, watched by other members of the royal family, the bridal procession walked slowly back to the West Door to the magnificent music of William Walton and Edward Elgar.

The bride's bouquet was made up of lilies, veronica, gardenias, roses and lily of the valley – all scented flowers. The only greenery was myrtle, traditionally carried by royal brides

A triumphant peal of bells greeted the newly-weds
as they left the Abbey.

Then, to cheers and shouts of congratulation from the watching crowds, Sarah and Andrew climbed into the coach for their return to the Palace.

The Duke of York and his new Duchess on their way to the wedding breakfast at Buckingham Palace

On the way back to the wedding reception, the Duke of York's new father-in-law, Major Ronald Ferguson, travelled with the Queen. His former wife, Sarah's mother, was in the following coach with Prince Philip.

Prince Edward had little success when he tried to keep order amongst the pages and bridesmaids in his coach.

The forecourt of Buckingham Palace – and the end of the beginning as the latest royal couple stepped down to start the celebrations with some lighthearted fun.

Another glimpse of that fabulous dress, too, that every other bride would wish for. By the following morning there were copies in every major city in the world.

Thousands and thousands of people waited patiently outside Buckingham Palace for the royal family to appear on the balcony.

The end of a
happy day

The wildly
enthusiastic crowds
packed around The
Victoria Memorial
encouraged the young
couple to make the
now traditional kiss

45

The photographer chosen by Prince Andrew to take the official wedding pictures shown here and on pages 48 and 49 was a surprise to everyone. He was Albert Mackenzie Watson, a top fashion photographer whose work has been seen on the cover of Vogue magazine.

The wedding cake was made by three Naval cooks at HMS Raleigh in Plymouth. This followed tradition, because Prince Andrew is a serving officer with the Royal Navy. An extra cake was made in case of accidents

A picture for the royal family album

Wedding group: Front row, seated, left to right: 1, The Earl of Ulster; 2, Lady Davina Windsor; 3, Lady Rose Windsor; 4, Andrew Ferguson; 5, Lady Rosanagh Innes-Ker; 6, Zara Phillips; 7, Prince William; 8, Laura Fellowes; 9, Seamus Makim; 10, Alice Ferguson; 11, Peter Phillips; 12, Lady Gabriella Windsor; 13, Lord Frederick Windsor. Second row: 14, Lady Sarah Armstrong-Jones; 15, Princess Margaret; 16, Princess Anne; 17, Princess Diana holding Prince Henry 18; 19, the Queen Mother; 20, the Queen; 21, the Duchess of York; 22, the Duke of York; 23, Major Ronald Ferguson; 24, Prince Edward; 25, Mrs Hector Barrantes; 26, Lady Elmhirst; 27, Mrs Jane Makim. Slightly behind them: 28, the Hon Mrs Doreen Wright; 29, Major Bryan Wright; 30, Alexander Makim. Third row: 31, Viscount Linley; 32, Captain Mark Phillips; 33, Marina Ogilvy; 34, Prince Charles; 35, Princess Alexandra; 36, the Duke of Edinburgh; 37, Princess Michael of Kent; 38, Princess Alice; 39, the Duchess of Gloucester; 40, the Duchess of Kent; 41, Lady Helen Windsor. Back row: 42, James Ogilvy; 43, Prince Michael of Kent; 44, the Hon Angus Ogilvy; 45, the Duke of Gloucester; 46, the Duke of Kent; 47, the Earl of St Andrews

Time to be on their way. Family and friends turned out in force to give them a right royal send-off with balloons, confetti, and a teddy bear – not forgetting that cheeky L plate!

And so, with the good wishes of all who know them – and many who don't – the Duke and Duchess of York start a new life together. No one knows what the future holds in store, but they are off – literally – to a flying start!

The honeymoon in the Azores

The honeymoon island of San Miguel

Acknowledgments

Designed by the Ladybird Art Studio under the direction of Roy Smith, Art Director: Liz Antill, Tim Clark, Nicholas Freestone, Graham Marlow, Howard Matthews, Stephen Pymm and David Swift; typesetting under the direction of David Miller: Roy Brewin and Stuart Morgan; bouquet for title page prepared by Ivan Eames, photographed by Tim Clark; platemaking by Leicester Photo Litho Service Ltd.

Photographs by courtesy of: Camera Press, pages 7, 8, 9, 22, 25, 33, 34, 46, 47, 48/49; J. Allan Cash, back endpaper A; Tim Clark, front endpaper (inset), title page, 15, and 19; College of Arms, 4 and 7; CPNA, 16, 24, 26, 28/29, 30/31, 35, 36/37, 38 (inset), 44, 45, 51; C. Evans, 15; Tim Graham, 5, 8, 11, 18, 20/21, 23, 33, 38, 40/41, 42/43, 44, 50, 51, and back cover; Anwar Hussein, 19, 21, 39, and 45; Metropolitan Police, 10; Mike Roberts, *Only Horses*, 8 and 14; John Scott, 4, 5, 6, and 7; Syndication International, front cover, front endpaper, 4, 6, 7, 9, 11, 14, 17, 25, 27, 29 (four black & white), 32, 47 (inset), back endpaper B (2); page 12 — research by *The Times*/Jenny de Gex, photograph by David Montgomery.

This book was on sale by Monday 28th July thanks to the speed and accuracy of Ladybird printers and bindery staff under the direction of David Collington.

British Library Cataloguing in Publication Data

Daly, Audrey
    Royal wedding, Andrew and Sarah.
    1. Andrew, *Prince, son of Elizabeth II,*
    Queen of Great Britain — Juvenile literature
    2. Andrew, *Princess* — Juvenile literature
    3. Great Britain — Princes and princesses —
    Biography — Juvenile literature
    I. Title
    941.085′092′2   DA591.A1

    ISBN 0-7214-0986-5